ON THE EVER-LOVELY MORROW

Fin Rose Aborizk

Edited by Flor Ana Mireles

1st Edition | 01

Paperback ISBN: 979-8-9906352-2-7

First Published May 2024

For inquiries and bulk orders, please email:
indieearthpublishinghouse@gmail.com

Also Available In
Hardback:
979-8-9906352-0-3

Indie Earth Publishing Inc.
| Miami, FL |

ON THE EVER-LOVELY MORROW

Fin Rose Aborizk

Edited by Flor Ana Mireles

1st Edition | 01

Paperback ISBN: 979-8-9906352-2-7

First Published May 2024

For inquiries and bulk orders, please email:
indieearthpublishinghouse@gmail.com

Also Available In
Hardback:
979-8-9906352-0-3

Indie Earth Publishing Inc.
| Miami, FL |

ON THE EVER-LOVELY MORROW

Fin Rose Aborizk

Praise for
AT THE BEGINNING OF YESTERDAY

"This poetry collection is absolutely stunning! Allen's prose is elegant, thought-worthy, and lyrical. A must-read, for sure."

~ Flor Ana, Author of *The Truth About Love*

"Visual, cryptic, and beautiful poetry, *At The Beginning Of Yesterday* has it all and everything in between. The reader is able to drift off into a world of mindfulness as each poem causes the reader to think. Reading the words of Tiffiny Rose Allen is easy, exciting, and meaningful."

~ Amelie Honeysuckle, Author of *What Once Was An Inside Out Rainbow*

"With every poem, I felt a release of my breath and an ease of connection. These poems were simply stunning, melodic, and human. This book is a true treasure to my shelf and heart."

~ Kendall Hope, Author of *The Willow Weepings*

"*At The Beginning of Yesterday* is a beautiful compilation of poetry that takes you on a journey of hope and forgiveness of the self that comes around full circle. The imagery and metaphors used by Allen ground you to the world and the universal moments we share. I am looking for the roots growing beside me."

~ Erin Flanagan, Author of *Haikus to Irish Tunes*

"Weaving femininity, the mystical, and evocative images in nature, Allen's work is not only ethereal, but empowering. It's the perfect book to gift your mother or your girlfriends."

~ Annie Vazquez, Author of *My Little Prayer Book: 75 Prayers, Poems & Mantras For Illumination*

Praise for
ON THE EVER-LOVELY MORROW

"*On the Ever-Lovely Morrow*, is...deep—though it's not a depth that one gets lost in. It's a depth that says, 'Hello, I am here, come explore.' This is the voice of a person who knows who they are, who knows that to be human means never to stop evolving, who has held all of the beautiful and uncomfortable parts of oneself, and who has unconditionally given love to each facet. This collection is beautiful! It's honest, bold, and romantic—all of the things that make poetry so lovely."

~ John Queor, Author of *Bypass*

"With *On the Ever-Lovely Morrow*, Fin Rose Aborizk explores the ties of past experiences to uncertain futures, all the while questioning the toll this takes on the present moment. This collection of poetry is a cabin in the woods, covered in a fog of nostalgia, a haven of cozy blankets and verses where you can stay the night while the world changes around you."

~ Renzo Del Castillo, Author of *Still*

"A beautiful continuation and stand-alone piece, *On the Ever-Lovely Morrow* explores the evolution of the human mind and spirit through the eyes of a poet. Aborizk lets us into their ever-changing mind in an ever-lovely way to show us that, despite all of our differences and truths, we may have more in common than we realize."

~ Flor Ana, Author of *The Truth About Love*

"*On the Ever-Lovely Morrow* is a book filled with intimate conversations that will reach your heart and words that will touch your soul."
~ Tammy Nguyen, Published in *Dreamer By Night Magazine* and
Dreams In Hiding Anthology

Continued Praise for
ON THE EVER-LOVELY MORROW

"*On the Ever-Lovely Morrow* is a lovely collection that is blessed with a whimsy feel that brings bliss to each poem."

~ Kendall Hope, Author of *The Willow Weepings*

"With great intensity, as recurring as the tide, *On the Ever-Lovely Morrow* offers round two for feel-good tears and smiles."

~ Keanu J. De Toro, Author of *The Eve of Our Generation*

"*On the Ever-Lovely Morrow,* just like its title suggests, is a journey to the center of yourself. It is raw in such a human and honest way, resonating with so many things I've felt but have been unable to express. Once again, I find myself at a loss to elucidate exactly how deeply the words on the pages have touched parts of my soul, reflecting things back at me like a mirror—a beautifully terrifying discovery. I have smiled and cried and so easily slipped into the vivid pictures and feelings painted by the words that come alive. Fin Rose Aborizk is a magical word weaver. "

~ M. C. Almaraz, Published in *Dreams In Hiding Anthology*

For Zachary,
For the music lovers, garden tenders, and ocean dwellers

"No one day is like another, each tomorrow has its special miracle, its magic moment in which old universes are destroyed and new stars created."

~ Paulo Coelho

"Love rests on no foundation.
it is an endless ocean,
with no beginning or end."

~ Rumi

"I am rooted, but I flow."

~ Virginia Woolf

Table of Contents

At The Beginning Of Yesterday

At the beginning of yesterday,
I loved you.

For to love was freeing so much more than my own choice.

To love was unraveling everything I had resisted and been afraid of.

Loving was beautiful and it was everything it needed to be.

That sunrise,

at the beginning of yesterday,
seemed to hold its hearts together.

Rightly so.

I waved at the trees as they began to rustle and sing,

and I think, what if we really are just stardust

spinning a web of magical uncertainty and fascinated glances through
telescopes and illusions of worlds and ideas set before us,

painting pictures with golden dewdrops of diligence and grandeur,

sophisticated anomalies and eyes staring straight into the same soul,

ON THE EVER-LOVELY MORROW

a union of fascination and peace,

a marking of a time that was profound and needed more than most,

the simplicity of a meadow,

blooming with daisies and pink wildflowers

while the wind tickled their petals and laughed, "Hello, my darlings."

At the beginning of yesterday, it was **ever lovely**, and beloved.

ver-Lovely Ever-Lovely Ever-Lovely
ver Lovely Ever Lovely Ever Lovely
verLovely EverLovely EverLovely
verlovely Everlovely Everlovely
verlovely everlovely everlovely
ver
     ever
          ever
               ever
                    lovely

This is where the poet came to dream

Ever-Lovely Ever-Lovely Ever-Lovely
Ever Lovely Ever Lovely Ever Lovely
EverLovely EverLovely EverLovely
Everlovely Everlovely Everlovely
everlovely everlovely everlovely
ever
    ever
        ever
            ever
                lovely

This is where the poet came to dream

It comes in waves. It comes in waves. It comes in waves.
It only ever comes in *waves*.

My Peculiarity

Tomorrow arrived and with it came another name,
a new name, and an old one.
A name that had a whisper.
A whisper of a name.
A semblance,
a glance,
of yesterday.
A glimpse unto yesterday.
A name that had been grabbed.
The clasping of a name.
A living thing.
A thing that was living
such was this name
This name was thus.
What a peculiar.
What a particular
present.

That's just it, isn't it?
That's just how it works.

You heal and then you rip open and then you heal and then you go through different things and different times and sometimes you have to reprocess and sometimes you just have to write it out. Over and over again. As many times as you need to, today, tomorrow, right now, forever. Will I forever be writing these lines? Am I only catching glimpses of the universe, glistening in my mind's eye?

Is this the place where I continue?
Is this how I continue?

The process of reinvention is often downtrodden, misunderstood, and perceived as attention grasping.

I hope that, when you look at me, you see flowers, flowers, flowers, flowers, flowers. I hope you see the ocean, and most importantly, I hope you see a friend that loves you.

The Scratching of My Palms

I've dealt enough with falsehood, I've dealt enough with fake friends and fake feelings, I've dealt enough with fake governments and fake food, I've dealt enough with the falsehood that comes along with a large portion of humanity.

Guide me towards the things that are good for me, point me towards the things that will make me feel. Lead me toward the shattered glass on the pavement in the parking lot, let me fall onto it and scrape my palms so that, as they are bound and healing, I'll know that, when I pick up my pen, I have felt the entirety of the world in the palm of my hands. Through the stinging of the cut, through the scratching of the bandage, I'll know that I have felt it all.

Point me toward something meaningful and true.
Something that is real.

*After Point Me Toward the Real by Ezra Furman

FIN ROSE ABORIZK

Let me be your rock of a poet.
There are worse things one could do in this world that is so unjustifiably full of suffering.

Let me speak to you of music, let me speak to you of movement, let me speak to you of water.

Let me speak on things that I have and have never spoken on before, let me lead you down the corridor,

the one that I feel I must walk down with you,
the one that I feel will make some things appear as if they are new.

ON THE EVER-LOVELY MORROW

"..Give Yourself a Present"

We're all a part of it.
The improvisation through life and doing what you can to find
happiness in the oblivion of days that twist and turn and circle
'round into the mundane and the exceptional.

It's almost like using the backing of an earring to keep the pins on your
jacket in place.

The backings always fall off but you find a way to keep them adorned,
showing them off, these little insights to your personality.
A little pin advising you to get yourself something sweet.

You know the one, it's that quote from Twin Peaks.

Just a Caterpillar

I know that I've seen you before.
And I know that I'll see you again.
And I knew that the first time I laid eyes upon you
that you were going to be there as I began to transform.

I felt that I was just a caterpillar when you knew me and now I am very
much eternally
something else.

If It Bothers You

If It bothers you,

It bothers you.

Briars

prior

to the thorn,

to the evergreen

to the little nuance.

A tincture,

cordial

different understanding.

I'm
thinking

It's
changing.

I've grasped the ropes of living and I've decided to follow it through.

No matter

the disposition.

No matter

how judged

I feel.

I wandered down the path, the hill,
and everything was turning out alright.

I didn't stutter, I didn't fumble, I just witnessed it for what it was

FIN ROSE ABORIZK

and I, well,
I realized in the silence that it was okay to be loud.

It was okay to be different or the same from yesterday or any other day,
and I detected and delighted in the fact that we are all just wandering
and doing what we can to feel and
find out where we need to be, as we should be.

I'd like to be like the flowers are,

the way they stand strong against anything.
A namesake.
A fond, futile emotion full of sweet perfume and a bumblebee
stopping by to whisper and tell me all its secrets.

I'd like to be how the flowers are,
a garden ever growing,

ever changing,

just like a small adieu

or a curfew after dark.
A singular little moment

of something to be present for.
And I didn't want your store-bought flowers.

I just wanted you to pick me wildflowers.
The ones you pass by as you walk,
the ones that make you think of me,

but maybe it's best that you didn't
because I always feel so guilty
any time I pluck something beautiful from its root.

ON THE EVER-LOVELY MORROW

Perhaps I am the Moth Now

The moth with its fluttered and renewed wings
scurries and flits amongst the tops of each stem of grass
in search of a wildflower just barely beyond its reach.

It's weird to look back because I feel like everything about me
has changed, and when I see you,
you seem to be just the same.

Why must I carry the metamorphosis of grief? Why must I carry it?
Did you happen to keep any for yourself?

Are we both just the same or are we truly different?
Have we both changed but somehow,
in our gazes,
are we the same as we were?

The moth wings aren't as loud anymore.
They fluttered near my hand, but
they've become so subtle now. Perhaps I am the moth now.
Perhaps its message has gotten through to me now.

There Was a Cadence in the Night

I open my palms as I stretch out my arms and
I can see all of the lines,
the curvatures and moldings—a fragment of my body
that ties to my soul.

My eyes trail down my arm and I notice the ink, the story, the placements.
I open my heart up to you,
I soften,
I fold, I'm sticky like glue.

But soon, I lay in bed and I stare at my palms, I stare at the ceiling and
I wonder
when I won't feel the way I feel anymore.
I grab the tissue and dry my eyes and dance around my room once more.

I stand up, I stand tall, I pack my things and I go,
I go, I go.

The city's veins curve as I go searching for, well, everything. The moon,
and Jupiter, waved to me as the wings drifted and the lights came into
clearer view, twinkling. Welcoming me. Telling me that the miracle
wasn't needed, for it had already begun.

There was a cadence in the night that opened up its arms and placed
something into my palms—the wanderlust of becoming nothing
but myself.

No Matter Where I Go

I'm so quiet when I travel. As someone who usually makes noise to cope with my surroundings, to feel more at ease, I have found that traveling lulls a lot of my social anxiety to sleep. There is no expectation of me amongst a group of strangers traveling along the same route. I am not an author, writer, or my day job. I am not the cat parent or the mommy- and daddy-issues friend. I am just a person, lulled to sleep by either the hum of an airplane or the wheels of a bus. I am just a person, experiencing the world in a way that is new, feeling peaceful in my contemplations, allowing me to focus and write down the things that I have come to learn. I guess you could say then that I am, in fact, the writer in this scenario. I guess I am always the writer. Forever finding inspiration no matter where I go.

How Could I Ever Find the Words?

How could I ever find the words?
Say it is as giving your voice to the sunset, embodying its beauty.
Giving your words to an image that cannot express itself in letters.
It's just
a feeling.

When the sun sets over the river,
it has us poets to lean on, to express through.
Or maybe, I am leaning on the sunset,
for without it, how could I ever find the words?

At Desert's Earth

Beauty does not hide here, it stands out in such a wide open space.

It's there, yet it is not demanding. It is simply offering an idea, a viewing as I look down to see quartz, and feldspar, and epidote on the ground—a natural occurrence of igneous stone, changed and rearranged from the time passing by.

I see the sidelines and I see the galaxies and what they said to me .

Bright shining,
glowing
florals—

the afterthought of afterglows.

I saw the little wagon,
the one with the broken wheel.

The loud assortment of better terms
and better ideological
ideals.

The wagon holds the flowers
as it creaks along,

jutting past the stones and the dirt on the road

to a
sedimentary
state of mind.

I Was Back in Miami

I'm exhausted, yet grateful, in Miami.
Water right in front of me and boats to wave hello to.
I've got to head to the airport 'cause I don't want to chance being late.
I want to browse the bookstores and call a lovely friend.
I want to take a nap and I want to lay in my bed with my cats,
but right now,
I am grateful to be here.

Coffee in Times Square

Sitting in a little coffee shop in Times Square,
about to go walk around a museum full of beautiful things—
solo
and
happy.

The Stonewall Inn

It was after the drag show and the drinks,
it was when you kissed her at the Stonewall Inn—it was the music
and the scene,
it was the taste of cigarettes and alcohol,
or maybe it was just the alcohol—but you danced
and you danced and then,
eventually—you kissed her goodbye.

Magnificence

So I sit and I ponder this life
and I wonder why we harm each other,
why we harm ourselves.

Am I so small that I don't see my own magnificence?
I loved to be by the sea
but where it is never mattered to me.

I just needed the waves,
the to and the fro,
the less and the low,
the more and the grow.

I wanted the sea.
I wanted the world.
Yet, too many stay too small to see
the idea of magnificence.

Thoughts on Doing Things Alone

If I fail at a plan or if something falls through, I know that I tried, I know that I continued, and I know that I have grown from it. Whatever the lesson that I learn when I am on the road, I know that each time I go, I will grow.

I Do Not Write

I do not write so that you may sympathize with me.
I write so that you may, perhaps, see a little bit of yourself typed and penned into a fragment of one of these lines.

I am just a vessel, grabbing words from another atmosphere and bringing them to you.

So when they tell me to *make sure you take your bc pills and keep your hair nice and long and don't walk too forcefully because you need to meet society's standards of how a woman should be!*

Perhaps I will meet my own standards.

The standard that I set for myself goes beyond the binary. Why are there only ever two perfect halves of something? Why not triplicates and quadruplicates and none-plicates? Why must there be a solid definition for a construct that societies paved to save their days and throw down others for?

A woman is often told to be settled, to be just one thing, but if a woman has a life, has a voice of her own, can't she be everything? Can't I embody just who it is that I am and leave the titles at the door? Can't it be enough that I live, that I breathe? Can't it be enough that I've longed for all the same things you have, too?

Perhaps I am just someone who does not want to follow the things that I have been force-fed.

ON THE EVER-LOVELY MORROW

I don't write my poems when I am surrounded by beauty.
I don't write when all is still and clear.
I write my words down when the catalyst has been switched on, when the rage is burning in me and I must put it down somewhere.
I muster up the beauty from the depths and I make it grow like a vine.

I write my words because I've got no other choice. I'll embody the flowers and the moths and the sky and the moon.

I'll embody them all.

I'll become them so that I might reveal my soul in its everlasting, ever-longing, ever-lovely way. I'll sing my medley for you. I'll envision and engulf all the love I've ever felt and I'll write it down when it is etched into my soul enough and rioted and rebelled and demanded to be set free. I'll write it down when it's taken me by my shoulders, made me pause and told me to listen.

It is at any point; it is with every backdrop and circumstance.

I do not write so that you may sympathize with me

I write so that you may, perhaps, see a little bit of yourself typed and penned into a fragment of one of these lines.

A Narrative On What It Feels Like When You Feel Like Everyone Hates You

I feel fine when I'm with people, cracking jokes and sharing every little thought that pops into my head, trying to make my friends laugh and make everyone's day a little bit better. I feel fine when I'm in it—

I feel fine when I'm in it.

It's when I leave and go home and rethink my day that the clouds start to set in, the thunder starts to roar and I think, *Oh my gosh why did I say that one thing and why did I say that other thing and why am I like this, and why am I like that, they all probably think I'm so annoying,*

constantly feeling like I'm some kind of burden, or someone who is simply tolerated. I really don't like this feeling, wish I could shake it from me, but I always feel like no one really wants to give me the time of day even though every day the love and companionship of my friends proves to be true and sincere. Sure, we all have our moments, and no one is perfect. In reality, I know that no one is really mad at me, and if they were, I hope that they would let me know why and so on.

Still, alas, I feel like I am constantly being bothersome. I'm just a little too much, a little too loud, a little too opinionated, a little too this, a little too that. It's rather frustrating. I annoy myself by thinking about how annoying I must be.

My brain is wired to automatically take the backburner of things: I

must be the one who's in the way, and I *must* be taking up too much space and I *must* deserve to be overlooked and treated like shit and have this constant feeling of inadequacy and just... Stop!

This mindset feels like it is rotting my bones. Some days, I am fine, and I know that I'm worthy of good things and I know that I am allowed to take up space and share my thoughts and my feelings. I know that I deserve good things, and I know that the people I love probably don't hate me, otherwise why would they hang out with me? I know that these bad thoughts will pass. They just seem to creep up and haunt me from time to time. An anxious ordeal that rinses itself off and then recycles its burdens with a fun little spin each time.

I've got to breathe through it and trust that I am loved and allow myself to feel and truly recognize the love that is shown to me. Sure, not everyone that I encounter will be good for me, but I can keep working on myself, and I can keep breathing, and I can keep on going, and not give up. I deserve good things, you deserve good things, and I hope that we both can find them at our own paces. Don't rush yourself, don't run, just keep walking, keep going wherever it is that you're going, and if that doesn't work, then just take a broom, sweep everything out the door, clear the air, and breathe.

Sticky Note Reminder

I grab my sticky notes so I can jot down updates and little reminders, and as I do,
that familiar feeling is making its way back to me, slowly walking over the sticks and stakes that I placed for it in my thoughts. Whispering in the background:

Imposter syndrome.

You know, throughout my life I was always made to contradict my inner knowing and I think that's why I second guess myself so much.

I'm not very good with rejection. I mean, no one is, so I rehearse in my mind and try to best prepare myself for the no's and the silences and the eyerolls and the people that think I'm showing off or being '*too extra*.'

One thing I like to tell my friends is "*If you have the opportunity to be extra, then be extra*," and I tell it to myself too, but I still feel like I'm just stumbling everywhere.

"Does anyone really care about my work?"

"Would anyone want to support an indie writer that they've never heard of?"

"Am I being annoying by talking about my creative endeavors?"

Just a few of the five million sticky notes that circle 'round this skull of mine. I feel like I'm too annoying, I'm not as qualified, and of course, it goes on.

I often worry about the future and don't remain enough in the present. I'm getting a lot better at that though.

I try to maintain the most optimistic point of view, but I still backtrack and spin around in a lot of ways.

I guess, at the end of the day, I'm just trying my best. I'm doing everything I can to feel worthy of... myself. And I guess my biggest sticky note reminder should just be pasted to my wall with these simple words:

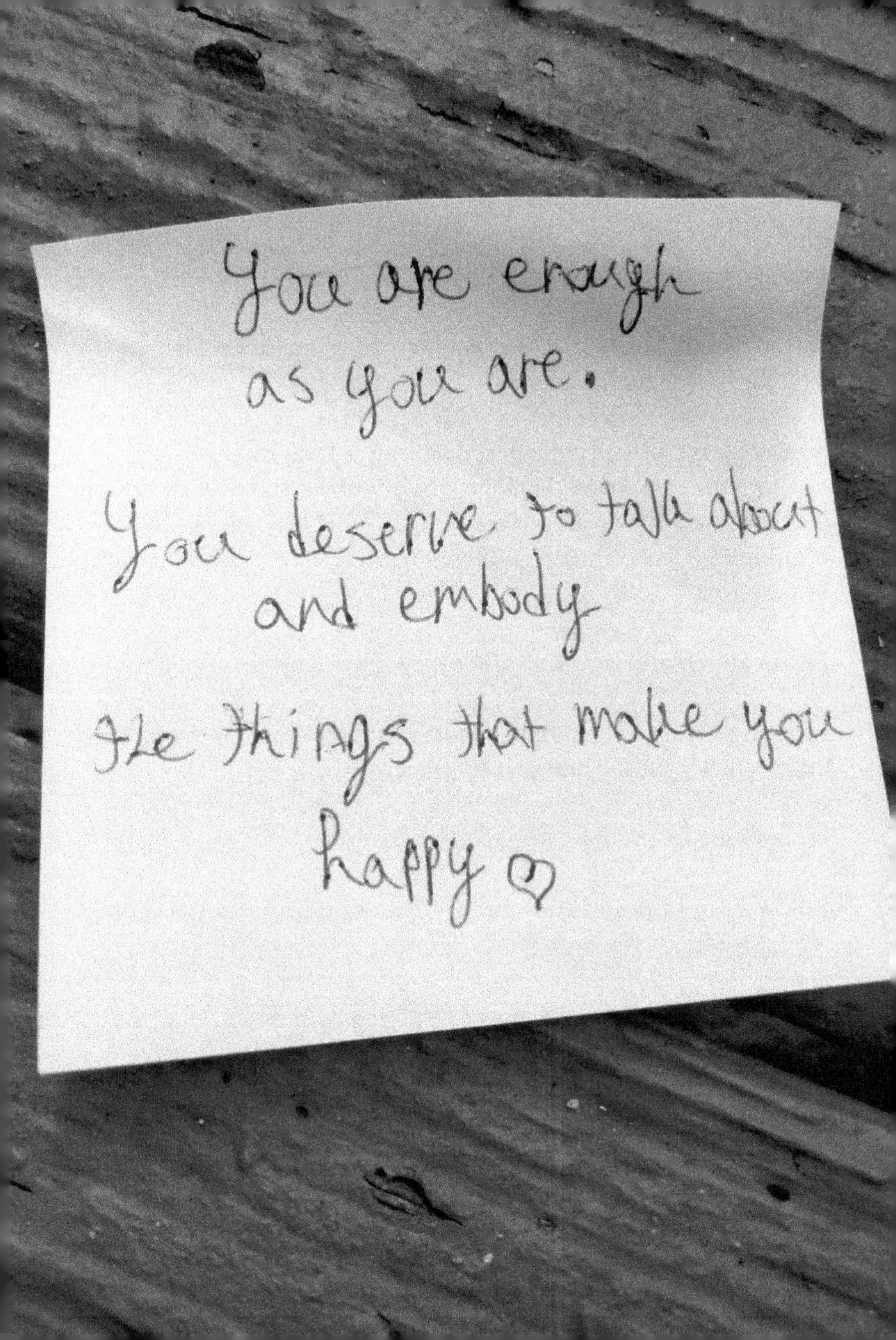
You are enough
as you are.
You deserve to talk about
and embody
the things that make you
happy ♡

ON THE EVER-LOVELY MORROW

Ever-Lovely

I always wanted to cut my hair but instead I was told that I had to
let it hang down
I always wanted to dye my hair but instead I was told that I had to
let it stay how it wa*s naturally*—

So as soon as I was old enough and as soon as I was really ready to
set down my own course, I grabbed the box of dye and then the scissors
and I became my own art project
of trimmings and colorings and layers upon layers of a different way to
be perceived.

My words spoke of my pain and my hair showed my joy—in a way.

I was never really one for fashion, but as time goes on, I just wear what
makes me feel like the best version of me:

my costume for the day.

I show up to work and I don't wear a lick of makeup, but the second I
leave, I adorn my face with gloss and glitter.

The more I grow older, the more I just don't feel a desire to be
particularly one thing or to be particularly one way.

I've always loved pink, but it is never the only color.
I always seem to lean more towards purple and yellow, and of course,
the deeper blues—

like the ocean when I'm gazing at the waves,
colliding and pushing and never, ever the same.

You might be able to say a lot about me, but one thing for certain is that
you will never be able to say that I have remained the same.

Maybe some of my mannerisms, some of my morals, and hopefully a
good or at least a fair sense of self-awareness but, I am always changing
and evolving and leaning more towards grasping that feeling of being
100% comfortable

as I am.

And I think that's really part of growing up, and I feel that the more we
change, the more we unravel the homes within ourselves.

My name is Tiffiny, but my friends call me Fin. My pronouns are what-
ever you can think of so long as it's laced with love. I consider myself
a woman and I also consider myself to be more—part universe if you
will, part of the ether that so many people still seem to be so afraid to
learn about.

And the more I express myself and the more I step into my truth and
the more my art project is trimmed and filled with each and every color
of the rainbow, with pockets full of crystals and bags full of tarot cards,
and poetry poetry poetry poetry everywhere,

that is the more that I embody love.

The more nonconformity is the more beautiful and brave and best and beloved.

How could I ever not believe in love, of any kind? For if I were to forsake the most magnificent of all feelings, surely that would mean that I don't believe in myself.

And I believe in myself. And I believe in you.

And I believe in the more expression and inclusivity, to have, to hold, and to honor.

It looks different for you and me, it looks different for everybody, and that is what makes it all so incredibly ever-lovely.

Bodi Bear

How lucky am I to have a little cat
that wants to sleep next to me at night, lick my arm when she's getting
drowsy, and then lay her paw across it as she doses off,
under the soft pets that I give her behind her ears.

Absolutely Nothing

I need to do the dishes.
I've got to clean this house.
I've got so much going on and it's funny 'cause I'm
keeping myself busy by
doing absolutely nothing.
So much I got to work on, and I'm so busy doing absolutely nothing
while at the same time doing absolutely
Everything.

Everything and nothing.

I had a dream last night
I was trying so hard to shake my love.
I didn't know why but I just stood there,
doing absolutely nothing and absolutely everything.

Everything.

Absolutely nothing, absolutely everything.

I'm doing absolutely nothing
and absolutely everything.

*After Chasing the Sun by Angel Olsen

A Day of Flowers

Today is a day of flowers.
I hear them laughing at my feet.
I hear them beckoning and beginning and quietly closing endings.

Footsteps answering and displaying a look of excitement and things to
look forward to.
I'm happy in this day and
not for any good reason.

I am simply taking in the breath of present tense and standing still. I
know what is meant for me will show.

I am no stranger to having to harbor patience even though I want to
rush.
I have to take it in slowly, deliberately, and straightforward.

We are not rushing the process.
We are watching through the window as the flowers dance in the wind,
knowing that they are taken care of,

the sun providing what they need.

Oh, to be a flower, outside in the sun, in the rain, in the earth from
whence we came.

Old Friends, Goodbye

It is so interesting to me how some people will only ever know a past version of you.

They will remember you when you were in a phase of unlearning, and even before that too.

Sometimes, no matter how desperately you want it, they will have no interest in knowing how you are now, and then again, maybe, sometimes, they will. It is so fascinating how we cycle in and out of different lives and different viewpoints, how we change from main character to side character, to stand-in and extra.

So, for the ones who I've said goodbye to either in words or in actions, I want you to know that I hold no grudge or malice. We more than likely just grew apart as people tend to do when they are growing up.

I burned my lavender,
just a few.
I burned for you.

*I've been building up my sanctuary, but I'm still missing
an important item from my altar.*

My Home State

I missed my Florida palms and I missed my Florida landscape
I missed that familiarity and the ways the roads stretched on
I missed how much it *felt* like home...

My home state
My home state
My home state
My home
My Florida highways and beaches
My seashells and gators and cicadas and armadillos

The nature here is honest
The nature here is honest
The nature
           here
                is honest

If you love something
or someone,
please
love it loudly.

I Guess

I guess I see the world a little differently.
I guess I've found that sometimes I've got to rely on myself a little more.
I might have a brother, a sibling, or two or three, and for that, I am thankful, but
I don't want to burden my sibling and my sibling does not want to burden me.

So maybe I ramble to the sky and I ramble to some friends until they get bored of me and I find some sort of peace in the internal cry, and I rely on myself a little more, and I write about it, and then I tell my therapist about it and

I find a way to manage it, I guess.

So much   time has
passed, is it   all different yet?

At the end of the day, it's all just a bunch of
words, and what happens to words when they
get wet upon printed pages?

They

bleed

and as they get washed away, there is room
to be left for more creation
when the sun reveals itself again.
More room for a burdened mind and
a spilling pen.

Every Way of the Ocean

There was always room for interpretation, if you would.
I wonder if I threw myself so far into my femininity that eventually my masculine traits had to peek through.

I can be soft and gentle and nurturing.
I can be strong and tough and brave.

Both ways,

either way, neither way, every way.

I can be nothing and everything simultaneously. I can be like the ocean. I can come and go in waves. I can process and heal within the tumbles of sea glass. I can wade and interchange and be a multitude within a current.

Maybe forced roles for one's identity are no more than schemes for ego. Maybe it is as stated in spirituality—for we are beyond our physical forms, after all. It took years of discarding the societal norms to realize that everything is *fluid*.

It took me a while to be grateful for it.

I didn't realize that the reason why I desired change so much and why one minute I felt one way and then the other

was because I was both and neither and none.

And so, what is my narrative?

I used to always change my hair and I always felt a shade of blue.

I think I'm like the ocean.
I think I ebb and I think I flow.
Today, I feel more feminine.
Today, I feel more masculine.
Today, I just am.

Most of the time, I just am.

I walk in a way
and I bring my laughter back day by day,

and I embrace the moment and how I'm feeling in it,
for it is valid all the same as it is true.

ON THE EVER-LOVELY MORROW

When All the World's Oblivion

The world is falling endlessly head over heels towards oblivion

and,
for a little while at least,
I got to a point where I just didn't care about being serious anymore.

I didn't care much about not smoking a cigarette and I didn't care much about not drinking too much, staying out late—I lived my life being so careful and, for once, I wanted to finally be able to just live.

The world is falling endlessly head over heels towards oblivion.

Please allow me to enjoy my concerts and my songs and my tattoos. Please allow me to enjoy the flower gardens and soft kisses, a moth landing on my fingers as a way to say hello.

The world is falling endlessly head over heels towards oblivion.

Maybe the poems that we write and the rhymes that we recite can save us all from dread,
can help us to know that hope is never gone.

I'll write about it a thousand times and a thousand more.

Hope is never gone for long.

When a situation I distanced myself from comes creeping up to haunt
me—Oh, how
I hate that anger, that feeling.
But God,

how it makes me breathe poetry.

Throwing the Leash

Every day I live, I realize more and more who I don't want to be like.

Someone hands you a leash and then they walk away; they don't come back and instead say that it was yours all along.

How can this be when it was always your own fantasy? How can this be when it's your name on the emergency?

I'm losing my mind. The cats are crying now. And so, I'm crying too 'cause no one wants the looks of you, and as much as I'd love to love you, I can't give you the love that you need.

So someone else cries and someone else denies, but just 'cause you've got more rings on now doesn't mean that you get to walk away from your responsibilities.

What kind of fool sees the rage building in someone, and continues to ignore it?

What kind of lack of self-awareness, to know you've deliberately chosen to turn your eye to something that only ever wanted to love you?

What kind of a person hates themselves so much that they don't give one single fucking shit how someone else feels about a situation?

What kind of a person, what kind of a devil?

You say it's all on me, but I never once asked for it. You just took advantage. It's on *you*.

And so, somewhere I wake up and I have more than enough money to do whatever I want and I have no debts to pay and no outstanding fees and I have a decent car to drive and other people's responsibilities aren't dumped onto me and I can give my cats a life of luxury and I can be happy just as I am. Without the expectation of doing anything for someone but just allowing me to exist.

To consistently set a boundary and have it taken like a twig and snapped in two,
then three, then four, then five pieces
is the breeding ground for insanity.

I just always feel like I am stumbling. It's not even so much a feeling of loneliness, it's more the feeling of being dismissed.

what to hold onto when you want to be rid of your mere existence

It is helpful to make yourself get out of bed.

It is helpful to make yourself clean your room, clean your house, and maybe even read a chapter or two from a book you've been putting off.

It is helpful to cook yourself a decent meal, nothing short of a sandwich, but feel free to shoot for something Michelin star level, too. It is even more helpful to drink water.

It is helpful to be surrounded by good people. It is helpful to find a community. It is even more helpful if you have a cat.

It is helpful to write about what you're feeling, even better to go outside to do so. It is helpful to do something that would usually make you happy, and it is helpful to try something new.

Yes, I know I've said it like fifty times already. It is helpful, but none of it is a cure-all.

A lot of the time after doing all of those things or only a few of them, you will still feel like *shit*.

The burdens in your mind will still crawl over you and make you retreat back to the comfort of your pillow and you will be stuck with no choice but to welcome it and give in. The pointlessness of it all will

envelop you and surround your senses and the rain outside will look like the perfect excuse to excuse any shard of hopefulness that might still be within you.

So why bother with the helpful tips if it all goes back to being how it was before? Why bother if my mind will always make me feel this way?

To be honest, I really don't know. I know it makes some great writing material though.

I'm only half kidding. I really do think you should bother because, well, the other day when I went outside with my morning coffee, I looked up from my cup and I saw a butterfly flying around the avocado tree.

I think it's important to bother because there is so much beauty that you've yet to see.

Things I Fall In Love With, Daily

Wildflowers on the side of the road.

The yellow flowers left outside on the doorstep welcoming the sun.

Discarding an old name.

Looking out at the ocean.

The adventure of discovering.

The beauty of becoming.

The love of releasing it all.
The love of writing it all.
Remembering everything.
Letting myself forget it.

Being still.

I let go of it, haven't I?

I embraced my name. I'm new now, right?
Why do I still think of it...
I think I've just peeled back the layers.

I haven't gotten rid of anything. I've just made it known.

FIN ROSE ABORIZK

Becoming, is exhausting,
but more so is stagnancy.

The things I fall in love with, daily, are
the things that scare me, the things that don't anymore.

The Scars That We Choose

When I went to get my first tattoo,
I got it as a present to myself.

I had a list of things I wanted etched into my skin and
I had a pattern and an order in which I wanted them obtained, but
one day,

I guess something crossed my mind and
all the while,
I was dealing with heartbreak on multiple levels, from family, romance,
and friendship.

So, I got a little ink and I got a little stain of
a scar that I chose—
tattoos are the scars that we choose, after all.

I got delicate flower petals adorned upon my forearm and I got words
to kindly tell me to *chill.the.fuck.out.*

Did you know that the moonflower represents our fragility, our mortality?

In a subtle time capsule of a moment, it all hit me and I decided

that was my piece to place upon myself
so **that I don't** forget about this body, this home, this life of mine.

And so, my friend told me he knows that I've been through heartbreak

and that it's written all over my face

and I have nothing to say other than pass me the vape.

Seafaring Rhymes

If I had to build a home in the sea,
I don't know what would suit me.
I'd like to say it'll all be okay
if I had a sword and a moment to pray.

I'd make friends with the pirates.
I'd help them find
the buried gold
and hope that they wouldn't mind

if I took some for myself so I could go upon land.
Just to pry and just to hear,
I'd see what the humans collected from along the sand
and see who it is that they all call their liege.

I'd open the barrier,
I'd walk, I'd play.
I think it would all be okay.

I'd make friends with the seahorse, I'd find the best starfish;
we'd go on so many adventures.

If I were to make a home in the sea,
I don't know what would suit me.
I'd like a tail, maybe long, maybe gold
and I'd like somebody to hold.

Something New

For all the time that I had been waiting, I was never really waiting; I was moving on.
 I was stepping forward and I was grabbing bricks to place upon each other,
and I built and I built and I built.

I saw the songs that moved me played out loud in venues.
I thanked the universe, I thanked the artist, I thanked myself for getting there.

I was no longer a clandestine fixture;
I was part of it, I was there.
I was dancing to the mushroom that played so loud, I was alive in the fortress of the bubble that was only a couple hours long.

And if someone else decides to become someone new,
 I'll know that I have become new too.

*After Mushroom Punch by Zella Day

I Like the Way

I like the way his eyes light up when he laughs.
It's a simple observation that puts the stars to shame and
all of the astrologers and matchmakers would say that it wouldn't be
quite right
but how am I to care when I like his laugh so much?
When I like the way he listens and the way he holds my hand...

Embrace the Current

I write up books from every dream I've ever had
and I continue to mourn the girl I used to be
and embrace the current version of myself.

I don't ever have to be just one thing. I don't ever have to be the same, and in saying that, I guess I also don't ever have to be different. But I think that as we change, we learn to do better for ourselves and others, and if we can be just a little more understanding, maybe we'll find something within ourselves that will allow us to be present in our joy and in our peace.

FIN ROSE ABORIZK

My grandfather when he told me why he put my name on the letter that he sent

My grandfather told me that it's almost like I'm in limbo until I can come home, or something along the lines of that. And I guess he was right. I did feel for a very long time like I was in limbo, and I guess I am finally coming home to myself, to what was always meant to be.
It was never my choice to change or revoke, but either way,
I am glad to embrace my name, a name that is as it was—a name that is flourishing.

There are a lot of things that my grandfather doesn't know about me, and that is alright.

There are a lot of things that he does know about me, and if anything, one thing I know is that I have done at least one thing to bring him joy, as he did for me.

He told me that I was worthy of my name; he reminded me that it was mine too.

Changed With Time

Then one day you realize that the name you were given was really just something that was placed upon you and it's not really something that feels like you, so then you go and pick a new name for yourself and it feels like coming home and somehow you end up going back to what was always yours. I don't dislike any name that I've ever had; I have simply morphed and changed with time.

Changing, is the one philosophy perhaps
that we can agree upon.
There is rarely a thing that does not change.
There is rarely a thing that does not stay the same.
The push of time is to preserve a past, but in doing so
it always in some way is *changed*.

It is human to gain a new perspective.
It is human to morph and dance
through the notes of time.

FIN ROSE ABORIZK

It feels like I'm in a world that I'll never really belong to.
If every dream is something I can make manifest...
if I'm to hold all my hopes in one hand,

I will always second guess where I am to place the other.

I want to disappear into the void of not being perceived or acknowledged.

I want to appear as the sun and be perceived and acknowledged.

Soul-Tied Cuisine

Fewer things make me happier than a meal that I've thrown together with my own two hands. An olive medley to awaken my palate—some mozzarella to remind me that it is okay to sit back and enjoy some of the finer things in life.

The milk and the cornbread, the tomato sauce and the soups, the discovering and the cookbooking and the finding.

Fewer things make me happier than the chickpeas and cardamom to dip my pita into, and of course, the lemon juice, to not let me forget that food is the sustenance of life, it is the energy source, and it is the foundation that connects us back to moments and histories.

Maybe not perfectly, but in my own way, it is how I honor the lives of the past that had a part in my existence. The reminder that we are all really connected over our plates, our family recipes and mixtures.

I am a medley of places and a compartment of recipes,

I am an improvisation
I am a delicacy.

 I am a piece of everything that made me,
yet I am
my own version of this soul-tied cuisine.

Time Well Spent

Could I have a cup of tea and could you maybe sit with me?

Could I make you some coffee and could we talk about the fashion of the 70s?

Could I make you sing again, not your voice but that's fine too? Could I make you sing again, the kind that's heard from the reflection in your eyes?

Can we be gentle, can we be soft, can we be a pillow, can we be a cloud, can we be a soft taffy, can we be a shared snack, can we be loving in the way that brings the laughter, brings the friendship brings the kind of things that makes us want to live each day for?

What To Talk About in Social Settings

It's not appropriate to talk about religion.
It's not appropriate to talk about politics.
It's not appropriate to talk about money.

It's not appropriate to talk about the things
that make the world go round and round.

It's not appropriate to discuss the wrongdoings of history.

It's not appropriate to talk about what you're seeing on the news.
It's not appropriate to talk about which gods you're praying to.
It's not appropriate to talk about the things that control this world.

God forbid we talk about it all and realize that some things should be changed.

God forbid we talk about it all and find that we're all quite the same.

Burn Out

I think I'm working myself too hard again.
Help me escape with my pen—
the blue one
with the ink that runs down the pages,
smearing its marks with understudies of ease.

You know the one—
how I took comfort in the sun, but it was always the moon that beckoned and called,
the duality of fixtures set up for my pondering.

The worry in its discontent doing what it does,
finding relatability in sadness,
but somehow looking towards optimism and fulfilled wishes.

I think I'm working myself too hard again.
Let me lie down.
Let me dream.
Let me hum the melody that is always stuck inside my head.

Love's always been a puzzle to me. I can't seem to get it right.
Like that time when I said, "really?" and you said "yeah."
But it wasn't really, and I wasn't mad.

ON THE EVER-LOVELY MORROW

Tell the Imposter to Go!

I find myself delighted as words pass through my lips, and then
I feel like I have always done something wrong, and
I feel as if I will never find somewhere that I will fit perfectly.

A blessing and a curse?

To never truly feel as if I fit only feeds my desire
for adventure and for travel, but,
 if I ever wish to stop,
 it is as if stopping keeps me away
from where I long to be.

I've always felt a little disconnected,

like I'm a power cord that just can't find the right outlet,

like I'm a puzzle piece that's forced to fit,

like I'm a dish lacking the right spice,

something that doesn't quite live up to its expectations.
And maybe my thoughts are all one-sided and maybe I'm just the constant imposter

unto myself.

What's the Point?

I think of what I've written and I think of what I've said. I think of every artistic thing I've ever expressed and I wonder what the meaning is.

What is the meaning behind everything I've shared? What is the point of it all? What is the purpose of ripping my heart open time and time and time again?

What have I to *give*? What have I given to *anyone*?

The only reason I can possibly exhume

is that I express everything I've ever felt because

I don't want anyone to ever feel the things I have

and not be able to find a friend to hold their hand throughout it all.

My words are my extension of myself, my condensed version of a hug—a joke told at the perfect time of day,

my plentitude of joy and my aches and pains.

Let me show you your pain and let me help you heal from it, for that's how I heal myself.

That's how I calm the storm and find the evergreen.

The point is in the connection, the point is in the line,
the point is in the song,
it's in the sky at evening time.

~

I think the true meaning of life is to help others, to be as kind as we possibly can be, and to love.

The soft coat of a puppy, holding a newborn baby, laughing uncontrollably, telling your friends to be as iconic as they possibly can be. Speaking out when injustices happen, learning, connecting. Listening to beautiful music, dancing through grief, hugs, watching your cats run around. Painting, writing, sharing...

Everything else is just...

FIN ROSE ABORIZK

The Process of Growing

I recount all of the mistakes that I made,
like when I was hesitant, and when I people-pleased to my own detriment...

But then, I remember how much I learned, how much I changed, and how much I grew.

I am never the same person as yesterday.

I truly do beat myself up for how immature I used to be, and I often forget that I've grown.
I often forget that I've shifted. I often forget that I'm allowed to be flawed. I don't have to be anything. I don't have to be anything.

I think too much, I think for not long enough, I think for every single reason and no reason at all.

And I think Gainesville is a modem,
I think that Albuquerque is where it all came to me.
I think that some names become outdated and others become reborn.
I'm not writing my words to try and show you that I'm a good person.
I am just writing my words to show you that I am, in fact, *just* a person.

This is just how I process my life—this is the process of growing and this is just how I move forward from things and this is just what I know.

A Life To Live

Only a fool would count how much life they've got left to live,
using markers to scratch checkmarks and times tables.
You desire to go anywhere in the world,
with a few dollars and some change.

You can disappear in the remnants of the planners
that you tore to shreds with all of your, well, plans.

You can get a new book to write into,
you can take it with you,
you can become a brand new thing.

You can calculate a new expression,
holding your favorite sweater close.

The marker boards have all turned into grocery lists and tic-tac-toe...
You chose spontaneity over fevered logistics,
you walked to the café just to walk to it,
you wore that jacket just to wear it because you didn't need to worry
then.

The calendar reset when it saw you be who you had always wanted to be.
We threw out everything that had a timer and we spent the time away,
finding joy where it was so often absent.

*After The Calendar Song by Laura Jane Grace

The Art of a Photograph

I sometimes think about photographers and how selfless they can be. I don't mean just the professionals or the novices; just in general, really. They take pictures of their loved ones and the flowers, the bumblebees and the water flowing effortlessly. They make it look like they've captured some magic, because, well, they have.

I think of how groups of friends go out and share some memories, thanks to the one behind the camera, taking candids on digital or polaroid. They get to keep those memories in a reminder of a still frame. And I wonder, you know, they save such gorgeous memories, but who is there to capture some of their magic? Who is there to photograph the photographer?

Photographers are selfless because I don't think they really think of themselves, you know? They think of the scenery or the celebration they're attending. They think of the beautiful moments being created, not how they look behind the camera.

I think it is a beautiful thing, but I also wonder if there is ever anyone there to take their picture, to show them how miraculous they look when they are caught up in their own moment, a moment of collecting a space
in time.
Granted, we have our selfies, but those are posed and deliberate; no less beautiful but not quite the same either.

It is no small thing to take a photograph of something beautiful. I don't think it really matters if it's taken on your phone or the world's best camera. I think all that matters is that it meant something to you.

It's a form of appreciation to photograph a thing.
I just hope that whoever is out there taking pictures of the night sky or their cup of coffee or the lovely architecture in town has someone with them to appreciate *them* too.

Rough Draft

I think we should validate the things that are seemingly left unfinished.

We push and pull the weight of building up and breaking down
and so often gloss over the in-between of being.

I lacked a certain course,
I took lessons, I began to sing my chorus, I
held unfinished thoughts and splattered them on paper.

I took my unknown recipes and headed straight for a disaster,
I lingered in the summer and
I charged ahead in winter.

I stopped writing when my ink began to bleed—
half thought sentences turning back into rivers,

my mind still picking puzzle pieces,
little fragments so I can create the sounds I'm feeling.

I don't know what this is all for and
I don't know… Maybe it will lead to anxiety or doubt.

In spite of every thread,
I keep on going,
pushing ahead in time and grace
'cause it's all just a rough draft, after all.

Writing My Own Waves

So this is just how it works. You're going to grow up without really wanting to and you're going to look at the celebrities and inspirational figures that died when they were your age and you're going to wonder and feel in awe at the legacies they left and how much they did while they were here with us.

You're going to ponder your existence; you're going to wish that you were never born and you're going to feel alone and you're going to feel forgotten—but then, you'll keep creating and then you'll keep on going.

You're going to have no idea how to handle your finances or how to do all of the things that real grown-ups do and you'll lie in bed and scroll on your phone all night and constantly daydream about what to do next and how to reach that dream inside your head.

Then, you're going to start showing up for yourself. You're going to put yourself out there and you're going to be ignored and some people will sneer at you and some people will laugh at you and some people will smile at you and you'll make wonderful new friends and have kind people who encourage you to share your life's poetry, for that's what this is—this is your life's poetry.

You could have written absolutely anything down and these are the words that came to you, and these are the words that you felt you had to share, and these are the words that became printed upon the page and distributed to who knows where, and hopefully, they'll have reached the hands of those who resonate and those who care.

You're going to keep going—like it or not—you're going to keep doing things, and you're going to keep loving, and despising, and raging, and desiring, and dreaming—and you're going to make it through.

Ponderings From My Bed

So the world begins to fall and it seems like life is relatively the same, except it's not.
I lay in my bed feeling awful, looking at news that is awful.

I think of how some people grow old and how everyone seems to die from something. No one seems to go easily, except a rare few and I wonder if my fate will one day be much the same.

I grew up with a lot of hardship and I often feel like I'm not fully out of it and I wonder if my life will turn into one of those fairytales—an ending full of happiness.

But then, I look around at the world and I see how fabricated it all is—how we destroy our planet, how we destroy ourselves—and I try to shake that story I read as a child from my head.

The one about a girl who was confronted by a witch, I think? Who asked her if she wanted to be happy in youth or in old age. The girl had chosen old age so that she could have something to look forward to.

And as I look around the world, all I see are reasons as to why fate will not lead us anywhere good. We have destroyed ourselves and those with no influence are left to watch it all unfold. But I hope it is just a nightmare that I'm having, and I hope I wake up to something beautiful, something good. Something that reminds me that *to live* is enough.

But is living enough if it leads to pain? What is it all for if we only have disease or disaster to kiss us good night? What is it all for if we can't find sanctuaries within each other?

I remind myself that a full life is not full because of how it's ended. It becomes full because of what we've done with our time. That is what makes it all become so deliberate and whole.

To Be Gentle

It is better to be gentle. Sometimes, it is better to forgive. Sometimes, it is better to lay the anger down after having let it pass over you—you *must* let it pass over you.

like a holiday where everyone has a board of charcuterie,
and you eat your leftover falafel over rice
with your coffee in a unicorn mug.

And as you type away and do the things you do on your computer,
you realize that you're quite content and
that there is always a little semblance of peace to be found.

Sticky Note Reminder II

So, a few things to make a note of:

All of the apologies that you're owed will probably not come to you. This should not stop you from moving forward.

To be present is to heal. To dye your hair and play your favorite songs over and over again. To type in your notes app as you wait for the timer to ring. To laugh at the fact that yesterday's pain changed you—hopefully into something better, but something else nonetheless.

I will never again be who I was; I will move on from it and then a wave will come and remind me, and I will continue on either way.
I want to rip the past off like a band-aid and throw it away, but I can't, for it has made me and I wouldn't want to be any different than the *me* I am today.

It all changes.
And we live so many lives and we love so many things and I want to move toward the things that make me feel like I am warm. I want to make others feel *warm*.

I will be okay with being just as I am.
Like the ocean, it will all come in waves.
I will always honor who I am meant to be.

After I've made my notes, I'll go and scrawl yet another sticky note reminder. This one will say:

Too Much of a Poet

I have given oceans to so many,
with only puddles and shallow pools leftover for myself.

So when the moon rose and the tides changed,
I had no choice but to rearrange
and let myself fill up with the sea.

My heart is too big, and I am too much of a poet
to not feel everything as much as I possibly can.

I remember what it was like to be numb and
I would prefer my heart to shatter than to never feel again.

What's That Phrase Again…Falling For Someone?

God knows I've desperately tried to be rid of this complicated heaven.

What should I do with you right now?
Is it wise to include the outcome?

Am I thinking too much into this?
Should I just go for it?
The world is
falling

        endlessly

                head over heels towards oblivion.

So why, why, why,

                why shouldn't I?

Why shouldn't I love someone?

Perhaps There Is More

That is just how life is.
That is our story.

We hang around a little while and then we go.
Perhaps there is more.
Perhaps again I will see the sunset, but
in case I don't, I will look upon the one in front of me and I will love it.

Just as I have loved you.
And to love you has transcended anything and everything that I have ever been.
To be still within myself has been the most beautiful thing that I could have ever achieved.

It has been more. It has been everything.

*After Be More by Stephen Sanchez

I don't want to move from a place of love.
I want to move *with* a place of love,
be a place of love.

I want to let the past know that I don't need to fight for my happiness
anymore—
I can just be it.
I can summon it any moment that I choose.

I'll Never Stop Believing in the Synchronicities

I look at the clock, and it says 1:11. I talk to my friend, and she just saw 555. So, I meet them over at 222.

I learn to be a little more patient, and I take every delay in stride—a moment I thought was going to be chaotic ended up becoming the very best.

Like when you meet on the solar eclipse, and then again on the 11th. The synchronicities align—and one can't help but wonder what the adventure is this time.

I'll leave you a sticky note reminder so it can brighten up your day.

On the Ever-Lovely Morrow

Yeah it was ever-lovely and beloved.
I looked so often to the past and I honored it so.
I looked unto yesterday and I thanked it, I thanked it.
I said so for my broken heart, I said so for my family's gaze, I said as I cried into the arms of love and doubt—it was all from another day.
And on the ever-lovely morrow,
I'll stand up from my meadow and I'll board my ship to sail
where the garden grows next to the sea
and the flowers tell the coral and anemone
that they are magnificent.

I will be a little kinder, I will be a little louder, I will try my very best, I will love, I will love,
for on the ever-lovely morrow, I will sail my ship, and I will look back and I will thank you.

I will see you on the ever-lovely morrow.
I will see you, I will see you.

I will see you on the ever-lovely morrow.
I will say my words, I will hold your hand, I will never let you be without a friend.

What Is More Poetic Than Carrying Dozens And Dozens Of Books With You?

I will always be the keeper of books, stories, and tales.
 I will always be the vessel for a word or two to pass through.
I will always be the poet, the little-too-sensitive word rhymer and free
verser.
I will always feel things just a little too deeply, and I will freeze
moments in time with my scratchings on paper.
With my typed and inked fingers, I will be home for the beauty that
is often overlooked and the metaphors that become our teachers and
keepsakes.

I will live, and I will travel,
on the big car or the big bird with wheels, going to and going fro,
with books in my bag and books in my hands
because I believe in the power that this life holds.

At the Beginning of Yesterday had two songs that I associated with it, those being:

My Love – Florence and The Machine
God Turn Me Into a Flower – Weyes Blood

~

The songs that I associate with On the Ever-Lovely Morrow as a whole are:

My Love Mine All Mine – Mitski
Vitamin T - KERA

~

The Music That Inspired the After Poems
These were the songs that I had listened to over and over during the course of this particular chapter in my life. Songs that were there when I needed a friend, songs that were there when I just loved the melody.

Point Me Toward The Real – Ezra Furman
Chasing The Sun – Angel Olsen
Mushroom Punch – Zella Day
The Calendar Song – Laura Jane Grace
Be More – Stephen Sanchez

Afterword

Suddenly, we've reached the end of this poetry collection. This one was heavy, much like all of the poems that I have written before it. I am a big believer in the saying that poetry is, in fact, not a luxury, and those of us who are born to be the givers of it are not the faint of heart. Granted, poetry comes in many glances and many ways, and poetry most certainly comes to those who are no strangers to perceiving in a form that is unique and eclectic.

Throughout this collection, poetry came to me very vibrantly through the songs that I had listened to. The After poems were the songs that were my travel companions, my background music, and my main character soundtrack. Of course, there are many more songs I could have written about, but these were the ones that I probably listened to the most during a specific period of time, which is why I was so inspired by them.

Bodies of water make me feel at peace and allow my mind to calm down, letting the gears churn so that verses can flow through. This collection is a declaration and a statement that life is in no way perfect, but somehow we can celebrate it in the little intricacies that are found within each day. When days get hard, we can still try to find a fragment of something to hold onto.

Healing comes in waves. Healing is a known thing that always surfaces and resurfaces. Progress can feel like it is unraveling and then going back and then unraveling and spinning and then illuminating everything all over again and then some. One thing I've realized is that no wave is ever the same, and sometimes, it is okay to jump in, sit with it, and then laugh as we splash the salt away from our eyes.

When I wrote *At The Beginning Of Yesterday*, it was the embodiment of a chapter in my life that changed everything. I knew what I no longer wanted to tolerate, and I knew that I had to stand up and allow myself to go after what it was that I did want and needed even. *On The Ever-Lovely Morrow* has been the continuation of what comes during and after, what comes when we have acquired the things that we held such a craving for. This collection represents the totality and accuracy of the fact that I am and always will be flawed, and that it's okay to move to and fro as life does the thing that it so often does, which is that of making us grow. The act of stepping into oneself as authentically as they possibly can, embracing my own experience of femininity, embracing the pushing of boundaries, and balancing all sides of one's essence and being. With a tomorrow that does not promise to be good, but promises to show us where we can go, where we should go, and where we will go. It must be enough to continue, it has to be enough to hold on and keep going forward, not backward.

I feel that it is my duty to try my best to find the magic in every single day, and with that comes more and more understanding of the human condition. The world is heavy, but there is still beauty, somewhere. That beauty is worth finding, and it is worth embracing and holding dear to oneself, and better yet, sharing it. So, this is me sharing the things that I have found to be both beautiful and heavy, gleeful and naught. Even so, it has all been what it has needed to be—and it warms my heart to know that you have read far enough to this very page. I hope you can feel the gratitude that I am emitting, because as I sit here and type these letters out with my very fingers, on my very hands, I am absolutely and incredibly grateful.

Acknowledgments

I would like to thank my publisher Indie Earth, and my editor, Flor, for being so kind throughout this whole process and helping me bring this creation to life. Thank you to my family, especially my grandfather, my siblings, and my friends for their support and words of encouragement. Thank you to Keanu, whom I would not have met if it weren't for our love of the art of wordsmithing, and thank you to every kind soul who has taken the time to read anything that I have dared to release into the world. I am always learning and growing and transforming, and I am truly so incredibly thankful for the people who have told me to keep going and to keep sharing. I would also like to thank those who were not as encouraging because without you I wouldn't have half the spite to keep doing what I do.

Thank you to my beautiful cats, Mama Kitty, Shungite, Bodi, and Dennis. My pride and joy. Thank you to the strangers who gave me the time of day at all of the markets that I have attended, thank you to the laugh that inspired a poem, thank you to the music that brought me solace when I was most in need of it, thank you to the food I learned how to cook that brought me some joy, thank you to the coffee that helped me power through my days, thank you to the outrageous most out of place thoughts that somehow found their ways into my head, thank you to my anxiety, and my rage, and my sadness, and my despair—thank you to my anguish and my joy and my love, thank you to every single feeling that we as humans can muster and embody and consume. Thank you for every flower petal, birdsong and raindrop. I am the most grateful I have ever been to have been able to rip my heart open and say *here I am*. Thank you for perceiving me and listening to what I have had to say.

Thank you.

About The Author

Fin Rose Aborizk is a writer, poet, spoken word artist, & overall creator. She began writing at an early age and entered the publishing world in 2017, where Dreams In Hiding Writing was born. Her first work is *Leave The Dreaming To The Flowers*, and with multiple poetry collections, a short story collection and an anthology of her own curation, Fin goes wherever creativity guides her. She has been featured in numerous magazines and anthologies over the years, and in 2023, *At the Beginning of Yesterday* was released with Indie Earth Publishing. Its companion collection *On the Ever-Lovely Morrow* was released in 2024.

In between writing, daydreaming about their next tattoo, and reading Rumi, she works on zines and shares the necessity of poetry however she can.

Instagram: @dreamsinhiding.writing

About The Publisher

INDIE EARTH
PUBLISHING

Indie Earth Publishing is an independent, author-first co-publishing press based in Miami, FL, dedicated to giving writers the creative freedom they deserve when publishing their poetry, fiction, and short story collections.

Indie Earth provides its authors a plethora of services meant to aid them in their book publishing experiences and finally feel they are releasing the book of their dreams.

With Indie Earth Publishing, you are more than just another author. You are part of the Indie Earth creative family, making a difference one book at a time.

www.indieearthbooks.com

For inquiries, please email:
indieearthpublishinghouse@gmail.com

Instagram: @indieearthbooks

Milton Keynes UK
Ingram Content Group UK Ltd.
UKHW021352260524
443099UK00015B/564

9 798990 635227